I Flunked Sambo University

10 invisible "schools" by which African Americans learn to look down on their own genetic heritage

David Hunter

ISBN:10:1541241932
ISBN-13:978-1541241930

DEDICATION

To all lovers of truth and
justice

TABLE OF CONTENTS

ACKNOWLEDGMENTS

Heartfelt thanks to Mr. Andre Robinson and Mr. Deric Felton for their thoughtful input and ideas.

I FLUNKED SAMBO UNIVERSITY

INTRODUCTION

Sambo University is the name I use for all aspects of American society that teach Black people to look down on people of African descent and rate them collectively inferior. The name "Sambo University" was inspired by the cruel, half Black overseer in Harriet Beecher Stowe's novel "Uncle Tom's Cabin".

The purpose of this work is to help sensitize Black people to some of the most subtle ways we come to see our racial kin in a negative light.

Sambo University, as effective as it is, achieving its unwritten objectives, is not a school of brick and mortar, even though schools that *are* made of brick and mortar have contributed heavily to the catastrophic mis-education of Black people about the Black race.

Sambo University's effectiveness is guaranteed by its ubiquity, which is comparable to that of oxygen. In other words, it is everywhere in our lives, penetrating and contaminating our conscious and unconscious thought patterns, directly and indirectly, as we breathe, grow, and reproduce. Unless we bury our heads in the sand, there is no way to avoid exposure to its pervasive influence.

And yet, the teachings of Sambo University are not necessarily deliberate or even consciously propagated. Of course, this is not to say that anti-Black agendas or anti-Black individuals don't exist because they most certainly do. Only a fool would deny their reality. But Sambo University, the bastard offspring of White supremacy and God-knows what other harlots of evil, has taken on a life of its own. It is now on automatic pilot. It does not need organizational propaganda to keep it alive. If every anti-Black organization and every anti-Black individual on earth ceased to exist tonight, we would still wake up tomorrow morning to the toxic teachings of this damnable institution. And, it will continue to poison Black spirits until we find a way to detoxify our own thought patterns and neutralize or resist its effects.

In an attempt to help awaken us to Sambo University's insidious assault on our psyches, I have broken it down into the following list of schools, which correspond to some of the major ways I believe we are taught or primed to hold our own racial kinsmen in low esteem:

1. **THE SCHOOL OF ANATOMY** or Eurocentric standards of beauty.
2. **THE SCHOOL OF HIS STORY** or recorded history according to Eurocentric historians.
3. **THE SCHOOL OF RELIGIOUS IMAGES** or images of biblical characters and Santa Claus.
4. **THE SCHOOL OF BLACK SELF-HATE** or intra-racial propagation of anti-Black myths, half-truths, stereotypes, etc.
5. **THE SCHOOL OF WHITE ON BLACK** or the suggestive influence of racist actions such as "White flight," police brutality, discrimination, White supremacist propaganda, racial slurs, etc.
6. **THE SCHOOL OF TARZAN** or

the unnecessary depiction of continental Africans as tribal and uncivilized.

7. **THE SCHOOL OF IQ ICONS** or the academic and informal exposure to non-Black icons (intellectual and moral), often and unnecessarily represented as globally and/or historically quintessential.

8. **THE SCHOOL OF PSYCHOMETRY** or the public knowledge of the gap in racial IQ scores.

9. **THE SCHOOL OF LANGUAGE ARTS** or the popular association of the word "white" with clean, pure, or positive things, versus the association of the word "black" with negativity.

10. **THE SCHOOL OF BARS AND STRIPES** or the visibility of the disproportionate number of Black people incarcerated, having criminal records, or being recipients of public assistance, etc.

The preceding list should not be considered exhaustive but rather representative of the multiple agents of Black self-hate/disrespect. It is hoped that it contributes to the overall aim of this book which is to enhance the visibility of Sambo University and inspire African and African American minds to resist its effects or flunk every course it has to offer, as I believe I have done personally.

Like all Black Americans, I enrolled in Sambo University at birth and I know for sure that its self-propagated propaganda is real and at the same time detrimental to our cause. I also know that Sambo University as I have defined it is invisible to many African American minds for a number of reasons including, but not limited to, denial, apathy, ignorance, naiveté, self-centered-ness, and passivity. These are the mindsets or frames of mind which make them great receptors of Sambo University's myriads of falsehoods.

As the book's title says, I flunked Sambo University, but I do not attribute my "failure" to any special endowments, not counting my seemingly innate aversion to injustice. Therefore, it stands to reason that other African American enrollees can do likewise. Even those who have already graduated can be detoxified with a certain level of determination.

This book is not an introduction to the

ways we learn self-hate, as I believe most Black Americans are basically familiar with the ones I have listed. My aim instead is to help make them easier to discredit by collocating them and giving each school a name. In other words, I am placing the "schools" on a sort of "most wanted" list. None of the teachings of Sambo University's stands up to logical scrutiny especially when one is armed with a certain number of easily accessible facts and information.

It would be ideal if Sambo university could be closed down forever, but if we can't close the institution we must close the apertures in our hearts and minds through which we intake the toxins it spews. I have no doubt in my mind whatsoever that on the successful side of such an undertaking is a better world for all.

Perhaps it would be a good idea if a structured curriculum, centered on these or similar listings, was developed to refute the teachings of Sambo University school by school. In the meantime, I have done a little refuting of my own at the end of chapters 1 through 11.

CHAPTER I

THE SCHOOL OF ANATOMY

<u>SUMMARY OF TEACHINGS</u> – Generally
Generally teaches that Black physical features, especially hair texture and skin complexion, are undesirable and aesthetically inferior to those of people

of European descent.

As a student of Sambo University's School of Anatomy, I failed ultimately to adopt the standards of beauty which favor people of European descent and apply them to my ratings and reactions to facial and bodily features of people of African extraction. It is all too often that Sambo University's honor students or Sambo Scholars (see glossary) thoughtlessly allow hurtful utterances that scar African American children, to fly from their mouths, oblivious or indifferent to the fact that the self-esteem of these young ones often hinges on their physical features.

Many seem to believe phrases containing words like "good hair" or "Black but beautiful" are innocuous or inconsequential. One does not have to be a trained psychologist to imagine that recklessly rating light skin, directly or indirectly, over dark skin, in the presence of impressionable minds, can lead to dangerous compensatory indulgences.

In some African American circles, the social air is often filled with commentary or toxic terms which send signals to Black children that pronounced Africoid features are unsightly. I have to keep reminding myself that most African Americans don't really mean any harm when they utter phrases that nevertheless wind up making children feel bad about their physical selves. Some of them simply don't know any better, because they are magna cum laude graduates of Sambo University's School of Black self-hate. In other words, they did not pay attention as anti-Black subtleties stole into their psyches, took up residency and started feeling at home. Keep in mind that those who are *not* paying attention or *did not* pay attention make Sambo University's best students.

As a southerner, I could literally recount thousands of anecdotes wherein I witnessed the spiritual blood of African American children being spilled, having been stabbed by stupid statements of the sort previously referenced. For me, the child's tears or the child's sad reflective countenance told the story of the effectiveness of Sambo University' pedagogy.

The high visibility of African Americans changing their natural features via cosmetic surgery, bleaching agents, etc. also send strong messages to both children and adults about the "inferiority" of Black features.

But we shouldn't be surprised that a great number of us swallow our racial pride and shamelessly alter our natural complexions in order to look like the overwhelming majority of people in this country. We are culturally pressured to both imitate the European phenotype and run from its African counterpart.

Where would African Americans have learned that straight hair or wooly hair are not universal standards and therefore, neither is "good" or "bad", or "pretty" or "ugly" in an absolute sense?

While some Black Americans will respond to American standards of beauty by straightening what is *on* their heads, others will somehow manage to straighten what is *in* their heads and leave it nice and wooly.

As an Afrocentrist, I naturally prefer the latter, but my aim in this chapter is mainly to point out that Sambo University's school of cosmetics, which teaches us to bleach our skin or chemically change our hair texture is one of the many battlegrounds that merits our remedial attention. As things are, the school adds momentum to the idea that Black is something undesirable.

In my weaker moments, I often shudder to think what other groups think about us or say about us, watching us doing things like parading blonde wigs, sporting Gheri curls, or purchasing bleaching creams. But I keep reminding myself of something I alluded to in my book "I hate Black people who hate Black people", our focus should be on what *we* think about us, and, what others think or say about us should be of secondary concern, if anything at all.

NOTES

Whatever effects of impressionable African eyes taking in the sights of our people bleaching their skin, wearing blonde wigs, or doing other things to look like *them*, is probably offset by the knowledge that *they* often do things to look more like *us*.

CHAPTER II

THE SCHOOL OF HIS STORY

SUMMARY OF TEACHINGS - *Generally teaches that Black people have little to no civilized history before contact with Europeans, which, in turn, reflects White innate superiority.*

Perhaps nothing else in our experiences as a people taxes our sense of wholeness as heavily as the exceedingly false idea that

Africa is, and always has been a place of savagery and barbarism. From this false premise it follows, that were it not for the slave trade, we, who are now civilized African Americans, would be running through the jungles of Africa today as half-naked spear-chuckers.

This has been the ongoing teachings of Sambo University although not in a direct way or as part of a formal curriculum. But indirectly, Hollywood movies, television, books, formally studied literature, and the very knowledge of our enslavement, all conspire to give so many of us the impression that we are indeed the children of an inferior stock of human beings, if not subhuman altogether.

At the same time, it was, and still is informally impressed upon us that the people of European descent belong to some sort of super race, typified by the likes of Einstein, Plato, Shakespeare, Edison, Napoleon, Lincoln, Mozart, and even Jesus. All of this was and still is reinforced by Hollywood or television in general, which consumes a big chunk of our willful attention. Even insurance commercials add to the problem and work against our comparative sense of worth.

At some point in my adolescent life, I

started to pay attention to the ideas propagated by Sambo University, which populated my brain with a forest of question marks. This, I attribute to the influence of my father who was never racially passive as were so many of his peers.

By the time I enrolled in college, my mind was ripe and ready for a healthy dose of Afrocentrism.

The first dosage came to me by way of a dashiki-wearing college professor who was even less passive than my father when it came to race.

The things I learned as one of his students would all but guarantee that I would fail to meet Sambo University's graduation requirements. Contrary to what Sambo University was teaching, I learned not only that we *too* had a civilized history after all, but that our civilized history was older and more spectacular than any other race on earth.

Having been inspired by the professor's Afrocentric interpretation of world history, I have read dozens of books that magnificently contradict what Sambo University tried to make me believe and confirm that precious little he smuggled into our brains.

But even if someone proved to me that all the cherished Afrocentric claims of Black scholars such as Cheik Anta Diop, J.A. Rogers, Ivan Van Sertima, John G. Jackson, Dr. Ben, and many others, including non-Black intellectuals, were indisputably wrong, I would still want to know what Herodotus, a Caucasian Greek, nicknamed "the father of history," was smoking when he described the Ancient Egyptians as "Black with woolly hair," even though his words were aiming to prove another point.

Plus, I would want to know, of what mental affliction did the "White" Egyptians suffer when they sculpted the face of the Sphinx to look like a full-blooded African.

NOTES

Knowing who we truly are, does not require a leap of faith, nor does it require hype, exaggeration, self-deception or anything other than an objective examination of the historical evidence. Not only does the evidence shatter the myths associated with our alleged innate inferiority, it does so in spectacular fashion.

As I said earlier, none of what is taught by the school of Sambo University stands up to scrutiny, logical or otherwise. Read the works of great scholars such as Dr. Yoseph Ben Yohannan, Martin Bernal, Dr. John G. Jackson, Dr. Chancelor Williams, Dr. John

Henry Clark, Dr. Amos Wilson, and many others. Study their writings and others like them and you too will flunk Sambo University with flying colors.

CHAPTER III

THE SCHOOL OF PSYCHOMETRY

SUMMARY OF TEACHINGS – *Generally teaches that the intellectual abilities of people of African descent are inferior to people of European descent, as demonstrated by "scientifically" designed instruments.*

Sambo University's School of Psychometry, more specifically, I.Q. testing, is one of the most dangerous adversaries of our quest to defend the human worth of the children of Africa. The very term "IQ" is so culturally embedded in or language until attempts to undermine it as real and valid might be looked upon with suspicion.

I do not mean to imply that I.Q. testing and I.Q. scores are rejected by all educated people because they most certainly are not. In fact, I would even guess that those who, like myself, reject their validity altogether, are in the minority (no pun intended). But my intent here is not to argue against the efficacy of the "science" of IQ testing (there's not enough time and space). I am rather citing it for the purpose of raising awareness of it as a legitimate threat to our spiritual recovery. It would be a colossal mistake for us to underestimate the damage it *has* done and the damage it *can* do to our cause.

If we sit still and do nothing, God forbid, we will witness, if we have not already done so, the imperfect science of IQ testing becoming the psychometric equivalent of a nuclear threat to the already-tentative belief in Black genetic equality.

It is not easy now, nor will it be easy in the future to persuade uninformed minds that the "science" of intelligence measuring is theoretically flawed, especially when certain social patterns seem to echo its implications.

I was tempted at first to believe that the racial gap in IQ scores is not known widely enough to warrant major concern that it might significantly fund the false idea of Black inferiority. I realized that it is much more visible that I first thought.

The underrepresentation of Black students in the so-called gifted programs announces itself loudly to parents, students, and school officials, who in turn, help spread the word that IQ testing is the basis of enrollment.

Popular books like "The Bell Curve" and the storms of controversy they tend to stir, no doubt arouse the suspicions of superiority-inferiority even in the minds of those who never read a single word that the authors wrote.

For what it's worth, I am perfectly confident that IQ scores don't tell accurate stories about comparative cognitive differences between humans in general, certainly not between the races.

The age old *nature vs. nurture* argument is still an effective speed bump against the relatively new science of intelligence testing. The claim that IQ tests are culturally biased against African Americans has had lasting appeal to Black Americans, especially because it is powerfully logical.

There are no two ways about it: Environment powerfully impacts the performance on IQ tests. Of course, Westerners seem a bit more willing to admit this when studies such as the one involving Ugandan babies suggest the exact opposite of what European racists prefer believing.

NOTES

The belief that God-given intelligence can be measured by IQ testing does not rest on perfectly solid ground in science or academia.

CHAPTER IV

THE SCHOOL OF IQ ICONS

<u>SUMMARY OF TEACHINGS</u> - *Generally teaches that the world's greatest minds, modern and historical (political leaders, inventors, writers, scientists, etc.) were of European descent.*

Since people of European descent make up the majority of America's population, it may very well be inevitable that White movers and shakers, historical and present day, are featured and glorified on a greater scale, quantitatively and qualitatively, than their minority counterparts. Even though this is not absolutely necessary, all moral appeals to change it would probably be a gigantic waste of time.

While it would be nice if academia and Hollywood voluntarily gave our African and African American geniuses the glory and attention Afrocentrists feel they deserve, it does not seem likely they will anytime soon.

But this is not just an idle complaint. It is

a reminder that we must concern ourselves with the School of IQ Icons's halo effect, wherein ordinary, run of the mill White folk, at least in some Black minds, are associatively cast in the limelight of splendor and glory attributed to European/American achievers, while faith in Black genetic aptitude shrinks in the giant shadows they cast.

There is no doubt in my mind whatsoever that Sambo University's School of IQ Icons nourishes the impression that people of African descent are inherently inferior. Since I don't believe in the efficacy of IQ testing, it is my opinion that objective world history or "unbleached" world history is the perfect antidote for the toxic effects of the School of IQ Icons.

Although I am not a formally trained historian, I know enough about what African and African American historians report about the distant past, to know that people of European extraction have nothing close to a monopoly on brain power.

Once again, it falls on those of us who have studied "unbleached history" to spread the gospel of what we have learned and encourage African Americans to follow in our footsteps and not be intimidated by the false impressions of "His story."

NOTES
J. A. Roger's book, "World's Great Men of Color" in one of many great answers to the IQ Icon problem.

Chapter V

THE SCHOOL OF WHITE SUPREMACY

SUMMARY OF TEACHINGS – *Generally teaches that the very existence of White racism, in and of itself, is evidence of Black inferiority (e.g. White flight, police brutality, discrimination, stereotyping, etc.) are merit-based and rational.*

The very practice of White supremacy, historical and present day, nurses the suspicion, if not outright belief, that Whites have a justifiable reason for looking down on people of African descent. This criminal idea is abetted by the fact that poverty, material and spiritual, afflicts a disproportionate number of African Americans, and cause some to act and behave in a manner that often parallels the stereotypical expectations.

While everybody seems to understand that White supremacy or racism in *action*, is detrimental to the lives of Black Americans, it may not have occurred to some that White supremacy as an *idea*, without arms and legs, *is* and always has been, harmful to our cause in very significant ways.

It seems very clear to me that in order to combat the dangerous and very real idea that being Black is inherently undesirable, we must either figure out how to turn all Black people into White people or validate, in African American minds, an alternative basis for the stubborn persistence of White xenophobia.

The former alternative obviously belongs to the realm of science fiction, but we are fortunate that science has given us a less shameful or more blameless basis, at least on our part, for White Negrophobia.

Let me pause here and explain that I use the word "science" in the strictest sense of the word because the science or scientific theory I have in mind is controversial and probably won't be welcomed with open arms by mainstream science for a long time, if ever. But at the very least, the "Color Confrontation Theory", as postulated by the late Dr. Frances Cress Welsing, easily meets the lexical definition of science regardless of how it is received by anyone.

It is worth mentioning that many great

theories of science were at one time met with derision and scoff by mainstream science when they were first introduced. But the great value I see in the Color Confrontation Theory, independent of its profound, thought-provoking assertions, is based on a potent counterclaim against the notion that Whites hate Black people for merit-based reasons.

Afrocentrists who have not already done so must recognize Dr. Welsing's theory as a weapon that can be used to help slay the dragons of doubt that attack our sense of worth on a daily basis.

NOTES

I believe the words of Albert Einstein, a German-American scientist of Jewish heritage, adequately demonstrate the justification for White on Black racism was manufactured by European minds:

"It seems to be a universal fact that minorities, especially when the individuals composing them can be recognized by physical characteristics, are treated by the majorities among whom they live as an inferior order of beings…"

CHAPTER VI

THE SCHOOL OF LANGUAGE ARTS

SUMMARY OF TEACHINGS – *Generally teaches African Americans to associate the word "Black" with negativity and "White" with positivity, thus reinforcing the "pigment figment" (see glossary).*

I have witnessed my brother on several occasions catch himself before using terms like "Blackmail" or "Blackball" because he knows that such words insidiously impact the myth of Black inferiority. He is certainly not alone in his wariness of the terms, as two of our most renowned leaders, namely Malcolm X and Martin Luther King, Jr., are among those who have denounced the semantic association of both terms.

So, like it or not, words, seemingly harmless words, that we use to express ourselves or simply convey a message, can contribute to the devaluation of the worth of Black people in the eyes of *Black* people.

The good news is that we can still express ourselves and convey messages effectively without using any words that associatively cast Black people in a negative light. But even if one is leaning toward the belief that such words have little or no impact on the way

Black people view the Black race, it still makes sense to refrain from using them unless it is deemed absolutely necessary. At the very least, by doing so, one demonstrates a very imitable loyalty to the Black struggle.

If that is not enough to persuade us to exercise prudence with anti-Black words, we need only look at the number of positive terms in the English language containing the word "White".

Is it possible to identify something as "White" and therefore "good" without implying that its chromatic opposite "Black" is bad or at least inferior?

NOTES

Perhaps we should consider refraining from referring to people of European descent as "White". If that idea has merit then we should use the term "African American" or "African" when referring to ourselves since neither black nor white is chromatically precise in describing any race.

CHAPTER VII

THE SCHOOL OF RELIGIOUS IMAGES

<u>SUMMARY OF TEACHINGS</u> – *Generally teaches that the alleged superiority and domination of people of European descent is divinely sanctioned, since virtually all biblical prophets and important people belong to that group.*

Race and religion have never run along parallel lines because parallel lines never meet. The lines of race and religion, however, intersect often, especially in the thoughts of Afrocentrists, most of whom were among Sambo University's worst students.

Afrocentrists worry that traditional depictions of Jesus and other bible personages tend to cast an associative spell over African Americans, inducing many to place unearned halos over the heads of people of European descent.

As one of these Afrocentrists, I share this concern, even though I find no fault in the teachings attributed to the Christ of the New Testament. But one of my problems with the traditional images is that they suggest that even the impartial, omniscient, all-loving creator God is signatory to the idea that people of European descent are inherently superior. The incomprehensibility of this implication alone is enough to cast a light of suspicion on the historical accuracy of the depictions and Christian beliefs in general. Yet millions of African Americans seem to content themselves with the idea that God is morally inferior to Democrats who at least politically embrace Affirmative Action.

But once again, it is a mistake to underestimate the power of Sambo University, whose teachings create Black automatons who question nothing except the rights of Afrocentrists to ask provocative questions.

As a result of the halo effect, many African Americans are looking down on other Black people. We are judging each other against standards that are not being met by anyone. White people don't turn the other cheek any more than any other group. In fact, many would argue that they do so *less* than any other group.

White people steal, cheat, curse, get drunk, swear, fight and turn against each other (look up the origin of the word "Balkanize"), neglect their civic duties, and cheat on their spouses with the best of them. They are also very late for important engagements and yet in the minds of Sambo Scholars (see glossary), they are the Teflon race. Nothing they do wrong sticks to them while every little African American infraction is amplified and interpreted as confirmation of God's creative "mistake."

NOTES

Nobody knows for certain what the people of the bible looked like. Some even doubt that many of them even existed at all. One thing we *do* know for sure is that it is highly unlikely that they bore the racial features often depicted. In fact, many believe the New Testament describes Jesus as a person of African ancestry. The parallels between Jesus and Osiris/Horus, African deities, are too striking to dismiss easily.

CHAPTER VIII

THE SCHOOL OF TARZAN POISON

SUMMARY OF TEACHINGS – *Generally teaches that Africa is and always has been a place inhabited by uncivilized savages.*

How wrong would I be if I assumed that most African Americans, especially those with college degrees, no longer think of Africa was a great big jungle, inhabited by half-naked barbarians? Keep in mind that we are well into the 21st century, separated by decades from the old Tarzan movies, which no doubt made a sizable contribution to the miseducation of African Americans about Africans in general.

But, how wrong would I be if I kept underestimating Sambo University's teachings to keep so many in the dark about the so-called Dark continent? Of course, old Tarzan movies are not the only culprit in this respect. It has accomplices in today's movies and television programs.

I would be hard pressed to count the number of times I have been shocked witnessing African Americans, especially ones with college degrees, being *themselves* shocked at the revelation that African has modern cities, airplanes, school, military forces, etc. I sometimes debate with myself as to whether or not to seize the moment and hit them with the "shocker of shockers" that civilization began in Africa or shock them with other Afrocentric nuggets of "unbleached history.

Material poverty deserves our sympathy and concern indeed, but I am much more sympathetic to the *spiritual* poverty of African Americans who see themselves as only a few hundred years removed from savagery and barbarism.

Pity the man who doesn't know where his

next meal is coming from, but pity more, the man who doesn't know where *he* came from.

Whatever self-esteem he has or thinks he has, is tentative, fragile, and resting on a weak foundation of superficiality.

As an African American who flunked Sambo University's School of Tarzan Poison, I not only know who *I* am, but I also know the true worth of all people of African descent. This is not a statement of pride but rather something close to a lamentation that so many of us are unnecessarily oblivious to our spectacular history.

If a certain amount of "unbleached history" makes its way into an African American's head, he or she will never again hang his/her head in shame of his African heritage.

NOTES

Contrary to what many unbelievably believe, Africa is not a country. It is a continent. It is not a jungle. It has sovereign nations, as do Europe, North America, South America, and Asia. It has modern cities with skyscrapers, cars, etc. And, by the way, the *first* cities in the world arose in the motherland.

CHAPTER IX

THE SCHOOL OF BARS
AND STRIPES

SUMMARY OF TEACHINGS – *Generally teaches that the disproportionate number of Black people incarcerated, having criminal records, or dependent on public assistance bespeak the innate inferiority of people of African descent.*

The visibility of the disproportionate number of incarcerated African American and those receiving some form of public support, speaks loudly in support of the false idea that we are somehow genetically predisposed to crime and other forms of deviance. Untutored minds often interpret the TV or newspaper images that correspond to the over-representation of Black people in these areas of deviance, as confirmation of the racist stereotypes.

But before one even dreams of putting crime statistics or any other indices on a comparative racial scale, mitigating factors such as poverty, over-policing, etc. must be factored in.

Of course, we might be naive to expect the Sambo Scholars and other students of Sambo University's school of bars and stripes to easily divest themselves of their miseducation and adopt the healthier point of view.

What do you say to a Sambo Scholar who has no idea that the racial gap which favors Whites in statistical comparisons of social deviance, shrinks dramatically when poverty, education, etc. are factored in the equation? What do you say to that 90-something percent of us (my estimate) who have never heard of the Dogon people of Mali (Africa), let alone that they live in a virtually crime-free society? If you find a place in America with a population close to a quarter of a million people with a near- zero crime rate, you have found nothing more than the Utopian dream of a Hollywood screenwriter.

What do you say to the sick Sambo, super students? I say: *Explain the Blacker-than-us Dogon people or explain why the statistical gap shrinks; if Black people are genetically predisposed to criminality, why do the Dogon people behave so lawfully?*

Furthermore, dare I dream, or is it asking too much that the Sambo Scholars also factor in the spiritual poverty that silently afflicts so many African Americans, regardless of education or socioeconomic attainment. In my mind, our spiritual poverty has a greater impact on our social issues than our material poverty.

NOTES

For me, the Dogon culture is the smoking gun or indisputable proof that Black predisposition to crime is real only in the mind of Sambo Scholars, be they Black or White.

CHAPTER X

THE SCHOOL OF BLACK SELF-HATE

<u>SUMMARY OF TEACHINGS</u> – *Generally teaches African Americans to openly express their incorporated anti-Black beliefs and teach other African Americans, including children, to look down on the Black race.*

In my book "I hate Black people who hate Black people" I introduced the term "Blackteria" which is defined as any Black person whose mind houses false and harmful ideas about the Black race. The Blackteria are further subdivided into three groups, based on varying degrees of disrespect for Blackness, namely, Malcolm vacuums, UnBlacks, and Sambos.

The Sambos are the Magna Cum Laude graduates of Sambo University. Their mastery of its teachings often manifests itself mainly in their unguarded moments.

Their Sambo University miseducation shines through often in the way they relate to other Black people, including even, their own children. Not only are they the best learners of Sambo University's false lessons, they are also its best teachers.

Of all Sambo University's schools, the School of Black Self-Hate is probably the most responsible for keeping myths, falsehoods, and half-truths about Black nature alive in Black minds. It ensures the intergenerational transmission of toxic anti-Black misinformation from grandpa to grandson, from grandma to granddaughter, and so on. It fuels the intra-racial propagation of negative ideas about Black nature that wind up taking a heavy toll on our confidence, the development of confidence, and, most importantly, it weakens the will to resist the past and present-day effects of White supremacy.

The School of Black Self-Hate is also responsible for creating the group of African Americans I call "unBlacks". My inspiration for the term is taken from old vampire movies wherein people who were bitten by Dracula were dead but didn't act dead and were often referred to as *undead*. The unBlacks are Black but they act as if there is no Black struggle.

By *Black* in this sense, I am not referring to the stereotypical conception of Blackness, but rather the dutiful consciousness that ideally comes with being Black in a world that questions the worth of Africa's diasporic children.

The great sin of unBlacks is silence, inspired by cowardice, indifference, denial, and God knows what else. They wrongly imagine that their racial inertia somehow insulates them from interracial adversity.

I almost never fail to notice how they shrink or slyly disappear when conversations about race reach a certain level of intensity. The great danger in the way they think is most aptly captured by the saying "A man who stands for nothing will fall for anything."

Malcolm Vacuums are also effective transmitters of beliefs and ideas that fund Black on Black racism. But the overwhelming majority of African Americans in this group simply don't know any better.

NOTES
We must do all we can, formally and

informally, to offset intra-racial anti-Black propaganda. I try to do this in my personal circle every chance I get, as tactfully as I can. For example, I bring up the Dogon people whenever there is a casual discussion of Black crime in a general sense.

CHAPTER XI

MISEDUCATIONAL MINDSETS

African Americans have responded to the teachings of Sambo University in a variety of ways. Most of the mindsets or thought patterns are detrimental to our struggle and have been harmful to our spiritual recovery. This chapter describes three examples of those responses and how they impact our quest for equality.

IDLE TITLES – or African Americans attaching themselves to religious or political titles for cosmetic reasons, while being indifferent or lukewarm to the moral or socioeconomic conditions adversely affecting Black people.

There are Black and White people in this country who believe their Christian duty is to *call* themselves Christians. Trouble is, the definition of a Christian, at least in their minds, matches up better with outward conformity than it does with one who emulates the Christ of the New Testament. Despite the fact that the New Testament itself clearly decries and denounces pharisaism, many in the clergy and the laity seem to treat outward conformity as an end in and of itself.

Although this brand of Christianity prevails in people of other groups, African Americans can least afford to ignore Christianity's true definition.

But Sambo University has taught us to place a high premium on outward signs such as churchgoing and doctrines that have virtually nothing to do with the lofty precepts and principles Jesus taught. It teaches us to gravitate to showy expressions of piety while being functionally indifferent to the moral and social issues that plague mankind, more specifically people of African descent.

It teaches us to use the church as camouflage for cowardice, selfishness, and apathy.

It even teaches some African Americans to embrace the bogus idea that the very resistance of racism/White supremacy is racist and goes against the will of God.

Lastly, it teaches us to allow religion to consume our thoughts, time and creative energies, which might otherwise be spent studying, reflecting, and conceiving viable solutions to our problems as a people.

It would be great if we tapped more into the pragmatism implicit in the apt little dictum "God helps those who help themselves", instead of helping those wretched souls who use God's name to help themselves to our hard earned resources.

Except for a few voices, there is a disturbing silence in our communities on the blatant trend toward religious hypocrisy and the mad rush of individuals to positions of leadership for selfish and often, ungodly reasons. As I mentioned in my book "I hate Black people who hate Black people", these individuals are taking up the space that was divinely scheduled for genuine spirits of change.

I am often surprised at the number of conformists in my circle who are privately disturbed by this hypocritical trend, but many of them are intimidated and silenced by the status quo and the superstructure of conventional ideas.

While there is no magic bullet for those of us who care, we must find the manhood to take verbal shots at the abuse every time the opportunity presents itself. I do it in private or casual conversation and in public speaking engagements.

PASSIVITY or many African Americans staying "inside the box", blindly conforming, winking at racial injustice, and accepting things as they are.

It is a tragedy of epic proportions that so many African Americans don't know the true worth of *knowing* the true worth of their genetic kinsmen. Not only do they not know, many don't believe there is anything worth knowing in the first place. Too many people shrug off or dismiss that precious little they hear by accident, as sensationalism, wishful thinking, or misinformation. As a result, they never examine the evidence or claims closely or objectively or dig any deeper than the Afrocentric words that fall on their ears.

This just goes to show that Sambo University has erected a thick firewall between the treasurable truths of African history, that might very well set us free, and the toxic falsehoods that tend to occlude our self-respect and erode our collective and individual confidence.

Confidence, which I believe to be indispensable for reaching full human potential, is much more essential than many apparently believe.

The roots of the "little" thing we call confidence run much deeper than is commonly supposed or imagined. It is, at the very least, not as evocable as the slogans and cute phrases we hear calling for its adoption, might suggest. Confidence is not as much the *presence* of something as it is the *absence* of something.

The confidence that propels people of European descent is not necessarily rooted in knowledge of their medieval and ancient history, it is simply unblemished by dehumanizing myths and falsehoods, at least from a popular standpoint. This is of course not the case with people of African descent.

There is no doubt in my mind that African Americans who earnestly and objectively examine the most basic Afrocentric claims would soon thereafter begin to see Black people in a whole new light.

The fact that many are disinclined to do so is the great challenge of Afrocentrists. We cannot stop and whine, as we often do, about their ignorance and delusions. *We* are the deluded ones if we expect a man who doesn't believe he is sick to want to get well.

If we don't succeed at redirecting their spirits, they will continue to cope by adopting nice, safe positions of neutrality, avoiding confrontation and conforming like hell to every popular tradition, be it efficacious or not.

Except we successfully intervene, their lives will be forever like liquids, always taking the shape of their containers.

Only a few in history have found the manhood to stand up to the bullies of tradition and orthodoxy.

Let us do all we can to help spread the fever that produces productive spirits such as Dr. Francis Cress Welsing, Marva Collins, and Dr. Alvin Palmer. These are examples of individuals who found the manhood to defy convention. Their defiance lead to almost unbelievable results and examples we should follow like the Magi followed the star of Bethlehem.

THE WHITE ICE SYNDROME or the tendency to habitually ascribe superior qualities to White people, their beliefs, values, and their enterprises, despite valid evidence to the contrary.

It is my guess that the old saying "White ice is colder than Black ice" was aiming to ridicule what was seen as anemic support of Black-owned business by Black consumers. But I think the applicability of the saying can be expanded to encompass any thought pattern in which African Americans blindly ascribe quality or righteousness to something solely on the basis of it White sponsorship.

Unfortunately, Sambo University teaches us to think this way about more than just business. The university's best students, Sambo Scholars, apply this way of thinking to a number of different areas including history and religion.

The teachings of Sambo University is what inspired at least one African American observer to say that Rodney King deserved the beating he suffered at the hands of LAPD lawmen. It would also explain why some of us take the provocative assertions of Afrocentrism such as the claim that Jesus was Black or Africans came to the new world before Columbus was born, with a grain of salt, despite lip service to the contrary.

Many Sambo University students will not dig any deeper or even give it a second thought when they hear or come across thought- provoking counterclaims of what I call "Unbleached History" (see glossary). Some of Sambo University's precepts are so deeply embedded in our psyche until contrary points are often met with scorn, indifference, or even ridicule.

Too bad, because almost all of us have heard or read about at least one of these extraordinary ideas. On the other side of the firewall that the university has erected in many African American minds, is a treasure of truths reaffirming who we truly are.

The evidence for many of these truths is supported by "smoking guns" which clearly show, for example, that the world's earliest civilizations have been bleached of blackness in the historical record.

It would be wonderful if all of us could mentally free ourselves of the white ice syndrome that hinders resolute inquiry into our spectacular past.

But since it probably won't happen like that, it falls on those of us who flunked Sambo University to spread the good news, not just about our unsung history and contemporary accomplishments, but also that Black ice is just as cold as White ice.

Knowing that one is under a spell is the first giant step from *under* that spell. Awareness, in and of itself, that so many of our minds are locked inside the White ice prison, will cause it to melt away. With a little more inquiry, the entire iceberg will evaporate into oblivion.

CHAPTER XII

THE SHAME OF FLUNKING SAMBO UNIVERSITY

As a student of Sambo University, I struggled to comprehend virtually all of its essential precepts. In my efforts to better understand the lessons, I naturally consulted fellow students who seemed to be grasping the fine points of its curriculum with relative ease. Some of them sympathized with my difficulties, but a great number of them looked upon my contrary viewpoints with suspicion, scorn and outright contempt. I always got the feeling that some even concluded that there was something wrong with me or my cognitive abilities. I was not that far from feeling something closely akin to shame as a result, harboring what some see as a somewhat warped world view when it comes to race issues.

I was baffled at first, but I found a measure of peace in realizing that I was up against an old, old body of counterfeit knowledge that had been ingrained into many African American brains, rendering many ready to defend a certain set of beliefs even at the expense of the respectability of their own genetic equality.

One of my favorite bones of contention is the idea of a Black racist. I do not contend that Black people *cannot* be racist toward Whites, I simply maintain that they are *not* racist toward Whites, and have not been for a long long time.

I suspect that thinking of Black people as racist has a sort of back-door appeal to some African Americans (bless their hearts) because it implies that we are in a position, at least perceptively, to look down on people of European descent. The infatuation with this notion, I believe, blinds us to the faulty or fanciful logic upon which it rests.

Another toxic idea being taught by Sambo University has to do with hair texture, a subject which has no doubt ignited many confrontational moments for Afrocentrists like me. Knowing that some African Americans are ignorantly wedded to the idea that "good hair" statements are innocent compliments, makes me hesitate to denounce them lest I sound foolishly overzealous.

I fight myself and keep reminding myself that such seemingly innocuous references are toxic slings and arrows of Sambo University's miseducation that should never enjoy free air time.

To hell with those misguided individuals who lump all interracial conflict under the heading of "racist", even clearly justifiable denouncements of racism or White supremacy. They make the stupid assumption that Black "racism" is perfectly analogous to White racism, which it is not.

I point out the "Black racist" and "good hair" issues to illustrate that Sambo University has its own built-in immunity system, which often silences pro-Black counterpoints and stands its sell-out Black defenders on the stilts of counterfeit morality.

CONCLUSION

The greatest source of power to be harnessed in our quest for socioeconomic equality is the "U-S" as in *us*, not the "U-S" as in the USA. In other words, instead of pinning all our hopes on government sponsored projects, including public education and legislation, we would be wise to invest more energy and thought to resurrecting the spirit in us that at one time, nourished the whole world.

It is imperative that we work to achieve a level of communal health that rivals or even surpasses that which animated us when we built the pyramids. But in order to have any chance of achieving this or any other level higher than today, we must first purge our souls of the spiritual toxins propagated by Sambo University.

It is my firm belief that a certain number of pre-legree and M-spirits (see glossary) will accelerate our march toward the equality we have pursued so long.

The force that is White Supremacy stands no chance whatsoever against the spirit that built the great civilizations of our distant past. External and internal threats would be rendered effete by a spiritually healthy Black America.

I am fully aware of the fact that the last two sentences in the preceding paragraph represent a gigantic leap forward across a great ocean of tears, sweat, and maybe even, blood.

But the treasures that lie on the other side of this vast ocean not only justifies my dream, it also justifies a vigorous pursuit of its realization.

The realization of my dream requires closing Sambo University, who foundation and walls are built on nothing but lies and mythology. The proven antidote for falsehood and misinformation is contrary, truthful information. It just so happens that almighty truth is on our side. We need only lead the flock in its direction.

There is an abundance of information, unassailable arguments, books, statistical data, etc. that disprove, discredit, and disable the teachings of every Sambo University school I have written about. Smoking guns for the surplus of lies, historical and otherwise, come a dime a dozen for open minds.

Every single school of Sambo University has been ably undermined by able Black thinkers for centuries, but many of their arguments are unknown to the masses.

This is one of the reasons I undertook the project of listing as many of the major ways Black people learn to look down on Black people as I could think of.

As things stand, the anti-Black schools of Sambo University float freely around us, undetected for the most part, yet slandering and defaming Black nature in Black minds. It is long past the time that Sambo University is systematically attacked, using the free and abundant ammunition granted us by the gods of truth.

Let us put the lies in our crosshairs. I love you, my brothers and sisters.

GLOSSARY

The following glossary of Afrocentric terms is pertinent to our struggle against the teachings of Sambo University. Most of them were coined by yours truly, while the rest have been circulated in our language for a long time, doing what I hope my newer ones will do.

I believe the terms, if popularized, will label our more insidious miseducational thought patterns and make them easier targets for pro-Black opposition and other remedial responses.

Aim-nesia – A phenomenon in which an organization, institution, program, church, etc. becomes focused on itself rather than its stated purpose, goal, aim, etc.

Backdoor complex – the tendency of some African Americans to stubbornly resist ideas, facts, and opinions that support Black equality.

<u>Backbone</u> – The courage and/or conviction to speak up for or champion a cause for Black people.

<u>Blackteria</u> – Any Black person whose mind houses false or harmful ideas about the Black race.

<u>Blancophilia</u> – Overweening admiration or respect for White people.

<u>Ebony Ebb, The</u> – The general weakening of the Black race or increase in its vulnerability to racial injustice.

<u>His-story</u> – (traditional term) The Eurocentric story or version of history, which many Black people see as distorted or falsified to favor Whites.

<u>IQ Icon</u> – A well-known White person who is regarded as a towering intellect or achiever.

<u>Malcolm Vacuum</u> – A Black individual, family, community, in which there is little or no awareness of or concern for the issues, values, etc. related to the Black struggle.

<u>Mama trauma</u> – The negative things parents, guardians, or other close relatives do and say to their young children that damage or tend to impair their emotional development, especially the development of confidence.

<u>M Spirit, The</u> – Strong proactive will to over or resist the effects of racial injustice, Eurocentrism or other threats to Black people.

<u>Marching Luther King</u> – A mindset wherein the individual possesses superficial knowledge of Dr. King's life, his philosophy, his views, etc.

<u>Pigment figment, The</u> – The imagined natural superiority of Whites or the false belief in Black inferiority.

<u>Pre-legree</u> – (as a Black person) Free of self-hate, race-based self-doubt, or having no doubt about the equality of Black people.

<u>Pygmalion effect, the</u> – (traditional term) An effect in which a teacher's expectations influence a student's academic performance.

<u>Sambo scholar</u> – A Black person who has an

extremely low opinion of the Black race as a result of the teachings of *Sambo University*.

<u>White ice syndrome, the</u> – A mindset wherein Black people habitually ascribe superior qualities to White people, their beliefs, ideas, values, enterprises, etc., despite valid evidence to the contrary.

www.ingramcontent.com/pod-product-compliance
Lightning Source LLC
Chambersburg PA
CBHW060227290526
45789CB00003B/1447